ORINDA

C 8

J392.36009
Lavine, Sigmund A
The houses the Indians
built

4.95

The Houses the Indians Built

THE HOUSES
THE INDIANS BUILT

Sigmund A. Lavine

ILLUSTRATED WITH PHOTOGRAPHS
AND OLD PRINTS

DODD, MEAD & COMPANY · NEW YORK

Illustrations courtesy of: Glenbow-Alberta Institute Photograph, Calgary, 60; Mexican National Tourist Council, 19, 20, 21, 22, 23, 24, 26, 28, 29; National Collection of Fine Arts, Smithsonian Institution, 63 *top*, 64, 69, 75; National Museums of Canada, Ottawa, 11, 12, 14, 58, 78 *bottom*, 79, 83; Plimoth Plantation Photo, Plymouth, Mass., 81; Royal Ontario Museum, Toronto, 51, 67; Smithsonian Institution, National Anthropological Archives, 49, 56, 63 *bottom*, 65, 68, 71, 78 *top*; USDI, Bureau of Indian Affairs, 8, 41, 43, 53, 72, 73; USDI, National Park Service Photo, 34 *bottom*, 35 *top* (by Jack Boucher), 46 *bottom* (by Davis Studio), 36, 37 *top* (by George A. Grant), 38 (by Parker Hamilton), 17 (by Homer F. Hastings), 32, 34 *top*, 35 *bottom*, 37 *bottom* (by Fred Mang, Jr.), 46 *top*, 48 (by Cecil W. Stoughton), and 31, 33, and 39.

Library of Congress Cataloging in Publication Data

Lavine, Sigmund A
  The houses the Indians built.

  Includes index.
  SUMMARY: Text and illustrations survey the homes built by various North and South American Indian tribes.
  1. Indians—Dwellings—Juvenile literature. [1. Indians—Dwellings] I. Title.
E59.D9L38   392'.36'0097   74-25524
ISBN 0-396-07076-0

For Al and Bill
who share the same "shelter"

C 8

Contents

Tepee constructed by the Takima of Washington State is covered with rush mats. Most people, when asked what kind of homes the Indians built, reply "Tepees." However, there was great variety in the shelters constructed by the different tribes.

1

"'Tis here they say the journey ends..."

Some 25,000 years ago, small bands of nomads following game entered the New World from Asia. Both hunters and hunted crossed from one continent to the other on dry land—the water that formed the Bering Strait was then held in suspension by the ice sheet that covered most of the Northern Hemisphere.

These Asiatic tribesmen and those who followed them became the ancestors of the Indians. Eventually, their descendants occupied North, Central, and South America. No one knows how long this took. However, we do know that men were living in caves in present-day Texas and Nevada ten thousand years ago. Actually, technicians can pinpoint with remarkable accuracy the year in which the Indians' ancestors reached a given locality, provided there is charred wood or bone at the site. They accomplish this by Carbon-14 dating. This process tests the charred material to determine the number of radioactive atoms (called Carbon 14, or C-14) it contains.

Carbon dating was developed out of the scientific discovery that not only do all living things assimilate carbon but also that certain of the carbon atoms taken in from the air by plants and absorbed by animals with their food are radioactive. Research has revealed that radioactive carbons are unstable and, as they decay, give off minute bursts of energy which can be detected by sensitive instruments.

Plants and animals stop ingesting C-14 atoms when they die and lose those that they have assimilated at a steady rate. Half of the radioactive atoms a particular object once contained have decayed at the end of 5,730 years. Therefore, scientists say that C-14 has a half life of 5,730 years plus or minus forty.

Thus, by measuring the radioactivity present in a given amount of dead vegetable or animal matter, it is possible to establish when a plant or animal died. Allowance is always made for error. Carbon-14 dates are written in this fashion: 6,400±. This scientific shorthand shows that the object tested died between 6,250 and 6,750 years ago.

Although carbon dating reveals that certain caves in Nevada were occupied for thousands of years, other caves served the first Americans as temporary campsites as they wandered through the New World. Skin tents and over-hanging rocks were also used for shelter in regions where there was little game. However, more-or-less permanent settlements were established in areas where animals were abundant. The dwellings constructed by the nomads were exactly like those their ancestors had occupied in Siberia—pit houses.

These shelters derive their name from the fact that they are partially sunk into the ground to provide protection from cold and wind. Those built by the first men to come to the Americas consisted of a hollow, approximately six feet in diameter and about a foot deep, scooped out of the ground. A frame of sticks or bones was placed over it. Furs and skins were then lashed to the frame with thongs, those nearest to the ground being weighted with stones, sod, or earth to hold them down. With the exception of a hearth in the center of the house, furs completely covered the floor.

The pit house was an ideal residence for nomads. Easily dismantled, its supports and coverings could be hauled from campsite to campsite during the summer. Moreover, if set up in sheltered spots and if enough fuel was available to feed their smoky fires, pit houses kept their occupants relatively warm during the winter.

Meanwhile, Eskimos living in what is now Alaska, who knew nothing of the snow-block igloo fashioned by their kin in the Central Arctic, developed stationary pit houses. Built over excavations three feet deep and ten feet square, they consisted of stone domes braced with whalebone and covered with earth. The latter acted as insulation, keeping out the cold and retaining the heat produced by a blubber lamp—a shallow vessel carved from soapstone with a moss wick. Although a very effective "furnace," much of the warm air thrown off by the lamp rose and collected near the roof. This is why the Eskimos fastened broad shelves on the rear interior walls of their houses about three feet below the roof, covered them with furs, and slept on them.

A crude pit house constructed by the interior Salish.

Igloo is the Eskimo name for a shelter, whether made of skins, snow, sod, canvas, or stone. This igloo is an example of the early ones erected before the white man visited the Arctic.

The summer dwellings of modern Eskimos are constructed from skins and poles.

In order to trap cold air and thus prevent it from cooling the interior, the house was entered by stepping down into a passageway, dug lower than the floor, which was closed off by a tightly lashed skin. Unlike many present-day housewives, Eskimo women living in pit houses had ample "closet space"—they used a small room off the passageway for storage.

Most early Alaskan settlements were small. However, archaeologists—students of past human life and activities—have unearthed the remains of six hundred pit houses at Cape Hope in northwestern Alaska. They were inhabited by the Ipiutak, a people who excelled in carving bone and ivory. Their town—one of the most extensive ancient residential sites known in North America—is the largest prehistoric community yet found in the Arctic.

Few of the original migrants to the New World remained in Alaska. Most of them fled the long, dark, bitter winters by moving south. Thus the tribesmen who permanently settled the Central Arctic were comparative newcomers to North America. They came from Asia approximately four thousand years ago. They brought with them skin boats and harpoons that enabled them to hunt seals and whales. They also had devised a wide variety of tools. But the best proof of their ingenuity is the igloo —one of the strangest shelters created by man. Although an igloo (the word means "shelter" in Eskimo) is constructed of snow it keeps its occupants warm even when outside temperatures drop to —40° F.

The technique of making snow houses has not varied over the centuries. A husband and wife working together can easily construct a family-sized igloo ten to fifteen feet in diameter in less than two hours.

Wind-pressed snow is the best material for making an igloo. Not only is it a nonconductor of cold because of its low moisture

Although built in the traditional fashion, this igloo has a glass window.

content but also it is not difficult to cut. Moreover, blocks fashioned from wind-pressed snow are solid and strong.

Construction begins with a "blueprint"—a circle drawn on the snow to outline the igloo's circumference. The builder then hacks rectangular blocks of snow about six inches thick which he arranges along the outline in a row that is actually a circular inclined plane. As a result, the succeeding tiers rise in a spiral. Each block is supported on two sides, the bottom and the edge resting against previously laid blocks.

Because the walls slope inward, the architect must stand within the circle facing outward and add blocks until the spiraling tiers close to form a dome. Incidentally, the Eskimo were the only people who discovered how to build a dome without using scaffolding.

Once the dome is closed, the builder cuts a hole in the side of the igloo and wiggles through it. Meanwhile, his companion has been plastering the outside with soft snow to chink cracks or holes. However, neither the small fur plug used for a vent in the roof nor the clear cake of ice or section of seal intestine that admits light is covered. This "window" is above the doorway which is reached by a tunnel built of snow blocks.

When an igloo is completed and furnished with a sleeping platform and a table made of snow blocks, blubber lamps are lit to "ice" the interior. Hot air from the lamps melts the spongy snow on the inside walls. When the meltwater refreezes, it not only glazes the inside of the igloo but also strengthens its walls and insulates them.

Shortly after the Ipiutak learned to carve weird animals and to whittle interlocking links of chain from a single piece of ivory, the ancestors of the Zuni began to settle the valleys of the Mogollon Mountains of New Mexico. These people lived in small pithouse villages. But their residences differed greatly from other pit houses. The holes, two to three feet deep, over which they erected their dwellings were as often rectangular as round. Sturdy posts formed the frame, saplings laid across poles served as the roof. Archaeologists believe that the entire structure was covered with woven reeds plastered with mud to seal the interior from the infrequent but torrential rains.

While positive proof that the Mogollons covered their homes with mud is lacking, there is no doubt that they lived in well-insulated houses. Although summer temperatures in the Southwest vary greatly, registering over 100° F. at noon and dropping close to freezing at dawn, they show little change throughout the day below ground level.

Although the Mogollons struggled to raise enough food, the ancestors of the Pima and Papago tribes were most successful farmers. These people, who are known as the Hohokam (from a Pima word meaning "that which has vanished"), built large earth dams to turn rivers into the network of irrigation canals that ran through their fields for miles. Because they had an abundance of food, the Hohokam could live in large communities—several of their settlements lie beneath Phoenix, Arizona. Huge pyramid-like mounds made of hard-packed clay on which temples were built were a feature of Hohokam towns. But despite these elaborate structures, the Hohokam lived in pit houses.

So did the Anasazi (Navajo for "the Old Ones") who dwelt to the north. The Anasazi—whose modern descendants include the Hopi—did not set their dome-shaped dwellings fashioned from logs cemented with mud very deep in the ground. But the most unusual thing about the earliest pit houses of the Old Ones is that they lacked an interior fireplace. The inhabitants probably warmed them by heating stones in an outdoor fire and then dropping them into a hole in the floor. However, later Anasazi pit houses had "central heating"—a fire pit and a hole in the roof through which the smoke escaped.

Incidentally, when the Anasazi began building pueblos, the first apartment houses, they incorporated the pit house into them. But the round, semiburied structures they constructed had masonry, not earthen, walls and were entered by ladders through openings in the mud-plastered roof. Very similar chambers called kivas are used today for religious ceremonies by certain southwestern tribes. The chances are that the Anasazi employed their partially submerged round rooms for the same purpose.

As indicated, pit houses not only sheltered the first Americans but also their descendants who migrated throughout the New World. But over the years Indians in various regions developed a characteristic architecture. In every case their dwellings met their needs and were made from easily gathered materials. Foragers and hunters fashioned various types of temporary or portable shelters from bark, brush, grass, reeds, or skins. Farmers erected sturdy permanent buildings from clay, earth, logs, or stone. Because agricultural tribes had to reside near their fields, their houses were close together. This, in time, led to the creation of towns that were surrounded with fortifications of strong pointed poles that served two purposes. These palisades protected crops from animals and the residents of the community from raiders.

Kiva (foreground) at Aztec Ruins National Monument, New Mexico

2

"The surest test of the civilization of a people...is to be found in their architecture."

The most remarkable structures constructed by any Indians were the clusters of stone buildings that often extended for miles through the centers of teeming cities in Central America more than a thousand years ago. Massive in size, beautifully designed, and gloriously decorated, they were the architectural equals of the public buildings in ancient Greece and Rome.

About 10,000 B.C., nomadic Indians following mastodons, mammoths, and other large animals entered what is now Mexico. Like their relatives in other parts of the New World, these hunters lived in portable shelters as they wandered. Then, about 7500 B.C., a climatic change caused the grasslands to dry up and the vast herds of game vanished. Faced with starvation, the Indians began gathering the seeds and fruits of wild plants for food. In time, they domesticated certain of these plants and settled down in permanent settlements.

Using irrigation to water their fields, these hunters-turned-farmers raised bumper crops. As a result, their population increased and their small villages became large towns. While trade was commonplace between these communities, so was war and,

Built by the Teotihuacano Indians about 2000 years ago, this pyramid, sacred to the sun, is one of the largest structures of its type in Central America.

eventually, the wealthiest and strongest cities established powerful states.

Among these were the Maya, builders of large cities in Central America. But their sprawling metropolises, filled with temple-topped, towering pyramids, wide squares, and palaces, had few permanent residents. The Maya lived outside their cities in scattered settlements. Their oval or rectangular huts, which were very similar to modern Maya dwellings, were erected on low earthen platforms to keep the floor dry during the summer rains. They had walls made of mud-daubed poles and thatched roofs. The latter also served as chimneys—smoke from the hearths at one end of the huts escaped through them.

The so-called palaces—long, low, multi-roomed structures—were normally used for storage. However, priests resided in them during their required fasts before conducting religious rites. Although the sprawling structures were "magnificently utilitarian . . . if anyone lived in them it was presumably for penance; they must have been very uncomfortable."

19

Abandoned about A.D. *1000, Monte Alban's buildings represent the cultures of three different peoples—the Olmecs, a group believed to have originated near Guatemala, and the Zapotecs.*

They were. Mayan architects were incapable of designing rooms that were not narrow, windowless, and high-ceilinged. This was because they did not know the principle of the true arch. They employed corbel vaulting. This consists of bringing the sides of two walls closer and closer together as they are raised until the gap between them can be closed with flat stones.

The great era of Mayan architecture began about A.D. 350 and ended approximately four hundred years later. During this time the Maya constructed numerous cities throughout Guatemala, Honduras, and Mexico. Then, in the 800's, they abandoned them. No one knows why.

Birds-eye view of the great plaza at Monte Alban in the Mexican state of Oaxaca. Here, the Zapotec Indians leveled a mountain top and built a religious center.

As the jungle enmeshed the deserted cities, other Maya living in Yucatan in eastern Mexico established an empire that lasted until the coming of the Spaniards in the sixteenth century. The artisans and architects of the "New Empire" did their finest work in the ancient holy city of Chichén Itzá. The stone structures they built were only one story high but gave the impression of being much taller because they were set on terraces or pyramids made of earth.

Working with stone tools, Maya masons filled Chichén Itzá with hundreds of public buildings, shrines, and temples adorned with the masks of gods, geometric designs, and brilliant wall paintings. However, while the exteriors of these buildings were magnificent, their interiors were no more attractive than those of the structures their kin had abandoned.

The most outstanding architecture in Chichén Itzá was created by the Toltecs who conquered the city in A.D. 1001.

Mayan pyramid temple at Chichén Itzá. Four stairways contain 91 steps each plus the platform on top to equal the 365 days of the year. Other temple features go into more calendric and mathematical detail.

Besides erecting flat-topped pyramids at Chichén Itzá, Mayan masons decorated stone pillars with masks, geometric designs, and representations of animals and birds.

Master builders, the Toltecs, traditionally the bringers of civilization to Mexico, had made their capital, Tula, one of the most magnificent cities in Central America long before they defeated the Maya.

Spanish chroniclers were impressed by the building skill of the Toltecs. One noted, ". . . their houses are beautiful, tiled in mosaics, smoothed, stuccoed, very marvelous." Another scribe reported that Toltec houses were "Built with consummate care, majestically designed."

Actually, the Spanish were not describing private dwellings but public buildings. The most remarkable were the temples constructed in honor of Quetzalcoatl, the Toltecs' chief deity.

23

Carved into ceremonial figures, these tremendous blocks of stone once supported a Toltec temple at Tula, north of present-day Mexico City.

The Itzáns adopted Quetzalcoatl under the name of Kukulcan and worked with their conquerors to build a huge residence for him. Set on a mound that rose one hundred feet above the plaza at its base, the structure was reached by four flights of balustrated stairs. Its roof was supported by towering columns depicting serpents and crowned human figures, while its walls were studded with intricate turquoise mosaics and representations of eagles and jaguars.

Over the years, the Toltecs constructed huge buildings, ceremonial sites, and colonnaded halls throughout Chichén Itzá. Under their domination, the city "rose to heights of prosperity, prominence, and architectural development surpassing anything in its earlier history." But most of its inhabitants fled Chichén Itzá about A.D. 1200 for some unknown reason.

Meanwhile, by war and diplomacy, the Inca of Peru were establishing an empire that eventually extended from Ecuador to Chile. During their early conquests, Manco Capac, a legendary hero, led the Incas to Lake Titicaca—the world's highest body of fresh water—which lies between Bolivia and Peru.

While his soldiers roamed through the ruins of Tiahuanacu, an ancient deserted city on the lake shore, Manco Capac closely examined its buildings which were constructed of cut, carved stones held together with copper clamps. Because Manco Capac realized that this method of building was better than the Inca technique of imbedding rough stones in clay, he assigned some of his soldiers to study the ruins and learn the secret of working stone.

They soon mastered the art. No people have built with stone with greater skill than the Incas. Lacking draft animals and wheeled vehicles, they hauled mammoth polygonal blocks from quarries by means of ramps and rollers to their construction sites. There, architects, who had fashioned a clay model of the structure being erected, supervised the placement of the blocks. Inca masons fitted cut stone with remarkable precision, keying each block to those on either side by rentrant angles—angles that are directed inward.

In time, Inca builders mastered the technique of using rela-

While excavating a subway right-of-way in Mexico City, a construction crew unearthed the ruins of pre-Columbian buildings.

tively small blocks cut to special patterns. Although they had no metal tools, Inca artisans shaped stone into any desired form. The ones they cut to raise the curving outer wall of the Temple of the Sun in Cuzco, their capital, did not move during a devastating earthquake in 1950. But a stone-and-cement addition built by the Spanish invaders tumbled to the ground.

While the Incas of the highlands built with stone, their kin on the seacoast used adobe (clay bricks hardened by exposure to the sun) to construct public buildings and their multicolored, gabled-roof houses.

Actually, most of our knowledge of Inca architecture has been acquired by a study of Machu Picchu, a fortress city to which the

Incas fled when Pizarro seized Cuzco. Then, when the conquistadors finally overran Machu Picchu, it was abandoned by both conquered and conquerors.

For centuries Machu Picchu—one of the very few cities of pre-Columbian America found intact—was forgotten until it was discovered by Hiram Bingham in 1911. Archaeologists have studied closely the city's numerous public buildings and private dwellings which are made of rough stones butted so closely together that it is impossible to jab a knife blade between them. Scientific investigation of these structures revealed that wind storms did not blow the thatch off their roofs—it was held down by stone rings.

Today, Machu Picchu is a tourist attraction. Women who visit the buildings that once served as residences for several families are particularly interested in the kitchens of these early apartment houses with their built-in grinding wheels.

In the morning we arrived at a broad causeway and continued our march . . . and when we saw so many cities and villages built in the water . . . we were amazed and said it was like the enchantment. . . . And some of the soldiers even asked whether the things we saw were not a dream.

Thus wrote Bernal Diaz, chronicler of Cortez's expedition to Mexico in 1520. The Spanish had good reason to be amazed at the sight of Tenochtitlan, capital city of the Aztecs. Situated on a marshy island in Lake Texcoco, the area now occupied by Mexico City, Tenochtitlan covered more than eight square miles and was jammed with sprawling blocks of one-story, many-roomed, terraced-roofed towers, pyramids, palaces, storehouses, religious centers, and other structures. Dominating the city was the temple of Huitzilopochtlo, the chief Aztec deity, which stood atop a massive pyramid.

27

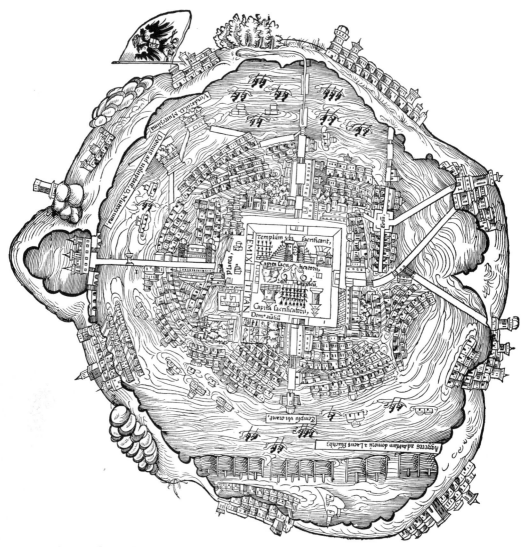

Cortez drew this map of Tenochtitlan, showing its temples, public buildings, palaces, squares, and causeways.

Sixty thousand people lived in Tenochtitlan. Another ten thousand lived close by. Many of the latter were poor and dwelt in thatched wattle-and-mud huts. The middle class in both city and suburbs resided in adobe-block houses. But public buildings and homes of the rich were made of cut stone.

Diaz reported that some of the Spaniards who had been "in many parts of the world, in Constantinople, and all over Italy, and in Rome" marveled at Tenochtitlan's avenues, concourses, and plazas. But their leader was most impressed by the canals that carried traffic throughout the city. That is why Cortez called the Aztec capital the "New World Venice."

Incidentally, the conqueror of Mexico was not the only explorer to compare an Indian community to Venice. When Amerigo Vespucci visited the northern coast of South America, he encountered tribes living in thatched pole huts large enough to accommodate several families. Because these dwellings were set on poles in swampy areas, Vespucci called the region Venezuela—Little Venice.

Model of Tenochtitlan, as the Spanish invaders saw it, displayed in the Museum of Anthropology in Mexico City.

3

"Build ye houses and dwell in them."

Fray Marcos de Niza must have been a very trusting individual. Otherwise he never would have believed the Indians who told him there were huge cities constructed entirely of gold in modern New Mexico. Fired by the friar's vivid descriptions of the fabulous treasures of the Seven Cities of Cibola, the Viceroy of Mexico commissioned Francisco Vasquez de Coronado to find them.

Coronado split his expedition into several parties and, as a result, covered a vast territory. But neither he nor his lieutenants found gold, silver, or precious stones. However, Coronado did reach Cibola. Pedro de Castaneda, who kept the log of the expedition, reported: "When they saw . . . Cibola, such were the curses that some hurled at Friar Marcos that I pray God may protect him from them. It is a little crowded village, looking as if it had been crumpled up together."

Actually, Cibola and the other "Cities of Gold" were Zuni villages built of stone and adobe. Castaneda thought Cibola was "crumpled up" because of the custom of married daughters' attaching their homes to those of their mothers. All the newlyweds had to do was to add three walls to the side of an existing building. This led to the development of a multiroomed community dwelling that housed an entire village.

Chaco Canyon National Monument, New Mexico, contains the largest of early pueblos.

Because of the size of these "apartment houses," the Spanish called them pueblos (towns). It is an excellent name as most pueblos were large. The ruins of Pueblo Bonito in New Mexico reveal that it was five stories high and contained more than eight hundred rooms. It was not until 1822 that an apartment house of comparable size was erected in the United States—the Spanish Flats in New York City.

Both men and women worked on a new house. Usually, the wife owned the family dwelling although her husband selected

Pueblo Bonito (beautiful village) in Chaco Canyon National Monument contained over 800 rooms and rose to five stories.

its site and decided its size. Next, aided by kin, he cut roof timbers, and then gathered stones and dressed them. Custom decreed that his helpers had to be fed during construction. Therefore, as few relatives as possible were asked to assist in erecting a new house.

Securing the roof beams was a difficult task. Timber was scarce and the fourteen-inch, ten-foot long logs had to be hauled over rugged trails by hand. Incidentally, archaeologists can determine the year in which ancient pueblos were built by matching the ring patterns of their roof beams with the number of annual rings in trees of known age. This system of dating is called dendrochronology.

After the men dressed the stones the women placed them in position. Women also made the roof and spread the thick layer of adobe that formed the floor. Evidently, children helped in covering the building inside and out with a smooth coating of adobe—prints of tiny hands can be seen on the walls of ancient ruins.

Because of raids by Apaches and other predatory tribes, the pueblo-dwellers moved their villages from the flat land near their fields to ledges on canyon walls as well as to the tops of mesas. They also built in caves. One of the largest of all early pueblos located in Mesa Verde National Park in Colorado is sheltered by a huge cave over 300-feet long.

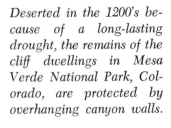

Deserted in the 1200's because of a long-lasting drought, the remains of the cliff dwellings in Mesa Verde National Park, Colorado, are protected by overhanging canyon walls.

THIS PAGE:

Left: Cliff Palace was built in the 1100's. More than 400 people lived in the structure, which not only had square and round towers but also underground chambers where religious ceremonies were held.

Below: The Square Tower of Cliff Palace. Built like a modern apartment house, Cliff Palace varies from two to four stories in height.

OPPOSITE PAGE:

Top: The ruins in Mesa Verde National Park, Colorado, reveal how the early cliff dwellers constructed their stone "apartment" houses along overhanging canyon walls.

Bottom: Two cowboys seeking stray cattle discovered the cliff dwellings that make up Mesa Verde National Park in 1888. This picture shows the largest cliff house in the park, Cliff Palace. It contains more than 200 rooms.

Ruins of the Wupatki National Monument, Arizona. Ancestors of the Hopi abandoned it about A.D. 1100.

At the time of the Spanish Conquest, the Hopi, Zuni, and tribes living in the Rio Grande Valley occupied some eighty towns, most of which were situated on high ground. All of them consisted of a single, many-storied structure containing apartment-like rooms. These communal dwellings rose in terraced tiers like a modern "wedding cake" skyscraper and either lined narrow streets or overlooked plazas. Not only did the steep-sided mesas—whose tops usually could only be reached by toe holds cut in the rock—provide defense from enemies but also houses in the lower story lacked outside doorways. They were entered through the roof by notched log ladders (pulled inside in times of danger) while upper floor rooms had either side doorways or hatches.

This interior view of the restored Great Kiva of the 12th-century pueblo at Aztec Ruins National Park, New Mexico, shows the pillars, roof beams, and altar room.

Stone work of the ancient artisans who built the town which now comprises Aztec Ruins National Monument, New Mexico.

Typical of the building sites of the pueblo-dwellers of the Southwest is the rugged terrain of Canyon de Chelly in Arizona.

In relatively recent years, many pueblo-dwellers have descended from their fortress-like villages and built new settlements on level ground. Among these communities is Zuni, a five-story complex housing some three thousand people. The inhabitants of Zuni—which was built on the site of one of the mythical Seven Cities in western New Mexico—hold their ancient Shalako Festival every year. During this celebration, masked dancers representing tribal gods bless new homes.

While Zuni is easily reached by throngs of tourists annually, visitors to the Southwest find it difficult to get to Acoma in Arizona. "A dizzy air-island above the plain," the home of the Acoma Indians sprawls for seventy acres across the top of a

The ruins in Canyon de Chelly National Monument in northeastern Arizona contain records of an ancient civilization covering a longer period than any other ancient dwellings in the Southwest.

straight-sided sandstone mesa nearly four hundred feet high. Acoma shares an unique distinction with another Arizona pueblo, the Hopi village of Oraibi, the oldest continually inhabited settlement in the United States. Both Acoma and Oraibi are the only occupied pueblos located on the same sites as they were when Coronado went looking for the Seven Cities of Cibola.

Late in the fourteenth century, dozens of pueblos were abandoned and forgotten until their ruins were discovered by prospectors, cowmen, and settlers. Because these ruins show no scars of war, it is believed that a prolonged drought, evidenced by narrow rings in tree trunks, caused their residents to move. No one knows if the inhabitants attempted to return when the long dry spell ended. If they did, they found their farmlands occupied by other tribes too powerful to drive away.

The newcomers were Athabascans—ancestors of the Navajo and Apache—who had drifted south from Canada. Armed with bows strengthened with sinew which enabled them to shoot harder and farther than the pueblo-dwellers, the Athabascans delighted in war.

There were really two groups of Athabascans, the original migrants having split upon reaching present-day Colorado. Those that went due south became the Apache; those that turned southwest became the Navajo. The Apaches continued to lead their nomadic life and, dividing into several small groups, supported themselves by pillage. Meanwhile, the Navajo, who had merged into a single tribe, became farmers.

During their wanderings, the Navajo lived in shelters formed from forked sticks covered with bark, leaves, or skins. After settling down they developed the hogan—an eight-sided, dome-shaped dwelling open to the east, fashioned from earth-covered, mud-plastered logs with an opening in the roof for a smoke hole.

Typical stone hogan found on the Navajo reservation

Originally, the Navajo built conical hogans whose "foundations" consisted of three upright forked poles locked at their tops. Additional logs were laid against the poles and then covered with mud or dirt. With the coming of the railroad, the Navajo often substituted railroad ties for logs. But the most radical change in building materials has been in the use of stone. However, the architecture of stone hogans is identical with that of the traditional "forked stick type" (which is still constructed), although many stone hogans have modern glass windows.

While some Navajos live in ramshackle wooden houses on their vast reservation, hogans shelter many of the tribe. Married couples usually build their hogans near the dwelling of the

41

wife's mother. This results in a small settlement of people bound together by family ties who cooperate in herding and house-building.

Every Navajo settlement contains several empty hogans—when an occupant of a hogan dies it is abandoned. General James H. Carlton discovered how greatly the Navajo fear Chindi, the god of death, when he attempted to force the tribe to live in barracks on a reservation. When the Indians refused to remain in any barrack in which someone had died, Carlton was forced to issue an order stating that the Navajo would be "permitted to live in their traditional hogans but these would be placed in uniform rows with good intervals and wide streets. One end of each row would be left open for Indians desiring to move. Then, when death struck . . . a family could move to the end of their row, where a new building could be erected."

At a very early date, most Navajo families built several hogans in different localities to shelter them while herding their sheep and goats from one grazing ground to another. But the marauding Apaches had no use for permanent dwellings. Their temporary camps consisted of wickiups—low, round huts constructed of brush and reeds which were covered with hides in the winter.

All wickiups are crude. However, those of the Paiute of the Southwest were mansions compared to the shelters built by their relatives whom Jeredith Smith, one of the most famous of Mountain Men, called "the most miserable objects in creation." These Indians lived in the Great Basin, a vast, low, dry area studded with deserts and salt flats. Because game was scarce in this region, the tribes who lived there had no permanent villages but roamed about in small bands seeking food. Until they learned to erect wickiups, they found shelter in caves or under overhanging rocks and slept on piles of grass or bark.

Actually, the flimsy, conical wickiups they made from willow or juniper poles covered with bark, brush, or reeds were the most primitive of houses and rarely kept their occupants dry. But food was far more important than shelter to these Indians. To satisfy their constant hunger they ate everything from seeds to roasted grasshoppers. But their staple dish was of roots which they grubbed out of the ground, the source of the name given to them by the settlers—"Diggers."

Meanwhile, in Arizona, both the Pima and the Papago were covering their dwellings with earth and mud. The Pima, whose villages served as stopping-places for wagon trains following the southern route to California, constructed dome-shaped pole and

Although this Yuma woman built her log-framed house in the traditional fashion with mud and brush, she wears modern shoes.

brush huts. Papago builders used the same materials to erect their round, flat-topped, thatched-roof houses. Wattle and daub were also employed by the Mohave, famous for painting and tattooing their bodies, whose lands extended to California. Mohave houses were square, low walled, and had flat roofs which were covered with brush and sand.

Certain southwestern tribes lived in open-sided, flat-roofed structures during the summer months. With the approach of winter they moved into rectangular-shaped dwellings with sloping sides. However, other tribes residing in areas where no snow fell stayed in *ramadas* throughout the year. Thus, long before architects began attaching an airy, shaded area to suburban houses, the Yaqui and other Indians enjoyed the comforts of a "breezeway."

4

"...And the mound-builders vanished
from the earth."

As trappers and settlers moved across the Alleghenies in the late eighteenth century, they were mystified by the vast number of earthworks they encountered. Some were only small mounds. Others were tremendous—one found near the present-day city of St. Louis was one hundred feet high and covered fifteen acres. Many of the larger mounds were formed in the shape of big birds or huge wiggling snakes. Others were towering embankments or steep, flat-topped pyramids.

Indians living near the mounds could give no information about them, but because ancient trees grew out of certain mounds, it was obvious that they had been built centuries earlier. This led to the creation of the myth of the mound builders—that the earthworks were the product of an unknown race whose civilization had been destroyed by the red man.

Although this belief was widely accepted, there were those who disagreed, among them Thomas Jefferson. He excavated a mound in Virginia and became convinced that it had been built by Indians. Then, in the late nineteenth century, archaeologists definitely established that the mounds had been built over a long period of time by various Indian tribes. Actually, the mound builder myth had been disproved much earlier. The

45

Mound in Effigy Mounds National Monument, Iowa.

One of the "Marching Bears" at Effigy Mounds National Monument. If you turn this page sideways, the white outline clearly shows the bear-like shape of the mound.

chronicler of Hernando de Soto's expedition to Florida in 1539 reported that the Indians of the Gulf Coast built the houses of their leaders on earthworks which they constructed "with the strength of their arms, piling up very large quantities of dirt and stamping on it with great force until they have formed a mound from twenty-eight to forty-two feet in height."

Archaeological research has revealed that certain mound builders had a highly developed society. But the first known makers of earthworks were simple foragers. Because a number of their mounds were found near Adena, Ohio, they are called Adenans. The Adenans' mounds were burial sites. So were those of the Hopewellians. Named for the owner of an Ohio farm whose fields were studded with mounds, they carried on an extensive trade throughout the Midwest.

Hopewellian commerce was eventually taken over and expanded by the Mississippians. These people dominated a vast area extending from Louisiana to Wisconsin and from Tennessee to Oklahoma. From the beginning of the thirteenth century to the mid-sixteenth century, the Mississippians were the most advanced group living north of Mexico.

The Mississipians, who probably traded in the Gulf region, were strongly influenced by Mexican architecture. As a result, they raised great flat-topped mounds on which they built temples and public buildings. The largest mounds were erected in vast cities with populations of twenty thousand or more.

Cahokia in southern Illinois is the most famous of these city-states. Located on a channel of the Mississippi River, Cahokia was the center of an area comparable in size to the State of New York. The city was completely surrounded by a palisade of thick logs plastered with clay, but its outstanding feature was the hundreds of mounds that overlooked plazas, market place, ball courts, and avenues. Some of the mounds served as storehouses. Others were used for religious rituals. Still others were ceme-

Those are not hills in the background but embankments raised by the mound builders in Iowa centuries ago.

teries. Towering above them all was an embankment with a base much larger than that of the Great Pyramid of Egypt. "Its sides are so upright," wrote a traveler in 1790, "that cattle can not get up on it to graze."

Over a thousand feet long and nearly eight hundred feet wide, the terraced mound was topped by a log-and-wattle temple with a steep peaked roof. There were other structures on the mound —its lower terraces were considered the city's most fashionable area. However, only those inhabitants of the highest rank were permitted to build a wood-and-brush house—its size denoting its owner's importance—on one of the terraces. Wealthy Cahokians of lesser rank had to be content with a residence on a smaller mound.

Carbon-14 dating reveals that Cahokia was occupied as late as 1550. But either continuous wars or a shortage of food caused the city to be abandoned long before it was seen by a European. However, various aspects of mound builder culture were continued by a number of southeastern tribes and observed by explorers, trappers, traders, and early settlers.

The Chickasaw, Choctaw, Creeks, and Natchez were only a few of the Indians who continued the ways of the mound builders. All of them were farmers living in permanent settlements that often had as many as two thousand houses within their boundaries. Usually, these towns were surrounded by palisades, some also had deep moats for additional protection.

While house-building was considered woman's work in most

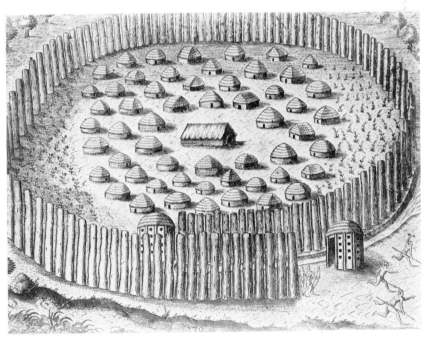

Old engraving shows construction of a fortified town by the Timucuans of Florida.

49

tribes, Chickasaw men, who were fierce warriors, constructed their families' houses. Each household owned three structures— a summer house, a winter house, and a storage building.

Winter houses were circular and had a diameter of about twenty-five feet. They were fashioned of framed pine logs and straight thin poles lashed together with either strips of bark or thongs. The roof, which was thatched with long, dry grass, and the walls were covered with mats woven of cane or flexible twigs. Both inside and outside walls were smeared with a plaster made of clay and grass which was painted with a whitewash compounded from decayed oyster shells, coarse chalk, or white clay.

Summer houses were rectangles approximately twelve by twenty-two feet in size and had gabled roofs covered with bark or grass. They were divided into two rooms by partitions and had attached porches. Like winter houses, summer dwellings had built-in beds whose frames of stout poles supported by short posts were fastened to the interior walls. Chickasaw summer residences were air-conditioned—small holes in the woven mats provided cross ventilation.

James Adair, who visited the Chickasaw in 1775, reported: "When they build the whole town . . . (they) assist one another. . . . In one day they build, daub with their tough mortar mixed with dry grass, and thoroughly finish a good commodious house." Adair also noted that Chickasaw towns had no pollution problem. Each family threw its garbage into a pit and covered it with dirt.

Natchez towns in the lower Mississippi Valley were domi-nated by two lofty mounds. One was surmounted by the large dwelling of the tribe's despotic king who was supposedly related to the Sun; the other was topped by a temple. The French, who exterminated the Natchez, were not as impressed by the tribe's architecture as they were by its caste system. Indeed, the rights and privileges of the tribe's hereditary aristocracy convinced French traders that the Indians must have had contact with the Old World before the arrival of Columbus.

But the more than fifty towns of the Creek Confederacy, whether they were residential communities or settlements set aside for war ceremonies or peace celebrations, astonished all visitors. There are several excellent contemporary descriptions of Creek houses. One of the best is in the *History of Carolina*, published in 1714:

> These Savages live in *Wigwams* or Cabins built of Bark, which are made round like an Oven, to prevent any Damage by Hard Gales of Wind. They make the Fire in the middle of the House, and have a Hole at the Top of the Roof right above the Fire, to let out the Smoke. These Dwellings are as hot as stoves. . . .

Painted in 1834 by Robert Petley, this water color shows the interior of a birch-bark wigwam.

The Bark they make their Cabins withal, is generally Cypress, or red or white Cedar; and sometimes, when they are a great way from any of these Woods, they make use of Pine-Bark, which is the worser sort. In the building of these Fabricks they get very long poles of Pine, Cedar, Hickory, or any wood that will bend; these are the Thickness of the Small of a Man's leg at the thickest end, which they generally strip of the Bark, and warm them well in the Fire, which makes them tough and fit to bend: afterwards they stick the thickest ends of them into the Ground, about two Yards asunder in circular Form, the Distance they desire the Cabin to be (which is not always round, but sometimes oval). Then they bend the Tops and bring them together, and bind their ends with Bark of Trees, that is proper for that use, as Elm is, or sometimes Moss that grows on Trees, and is a Yard or two long, and never rots; then they brace them with other Poles to make them strong; afterwards cover them all over with Bark, so that they are very warm and tight, and will keep firm against all the weathers that blow. They have other sorts of cabins without windows, which are for their Granaries, Skins, and Merchandizes; and others that are covered overhead; the rest left open for the Air. These have Reed-Hurdles like Tables to lie and sit on, in Summer, and serve for pleasant Banqueting-Houses in the hot Season of the Year.

The dome-shaped, seven-sided houses in Cherokee villages are also mentioned by early travelers. So are the dwellings of the Seminoles. These Indians built open-sided, palmetto-thatched huts which stood on two-foot tall sticks to keep their floors dry in the rainy season. According to the author of *The Whole and True Discoverye of Terra Florida* (1563), Seminole houses were constructed "like a pavilion."

The Seminoles still carry on their old ways in the Everglades of Florida.

Incidentally, Seminoles living in the Florida Everglades—a region consisting of too much water to be land and too much land to be water—still build "pavilions." But the descendants of those members of the tribe that were forced onto an Oklahoma reservation in 1842 after a long and bitter struggle construct log cabins.

5

"The house shows the owner."

In recent years, shrewd real estate developers and Chambers of Commerce have lured thousands of people to California. They have done this by stressing the state's delightful climate. The chances are that if one of their brochures could have been read by the Chumush, Hupa, Maidu, Yurok, and other Indians who lived there a century or so ago, the red men would have agreed with every word. These tribes had settled in California because of its mild climate. They had also been attracted by its rich plant and animal life.

California tribes were small but numerous. In fact, before the coming of the white man, California was the home of "one of the largest and most varied concentrations of Indians north of Mexico," and more Indian languages were spoken there than anywhere else.

There was just as much variation in the architecture of the region as there was in its speech. Some tribes built dome- or conical-shaped houses from poles and covered them with bark, brush, earth, rush mats, or wooden slabs. Others, including the Maidu of the Sacramento Valley, lived in villages composed of large earthen lodges. Still others covered their round, domed dwellings with a plaster of adobe or mud. The Indians who inhabited the area near the present-day fashionable desert resort of

Palm Springs fashioned their homes from palm fronds.

However, the Pomo—who wove baskets so tightly that they held water—employed the most easily gathered material available when constructing the houses in their seventy-odd villages. As a result, Pomo bands living near the sea built houses by leaning large slabs of redwood bark against heavy timbers to form a cone six-to-eight feet high and ten-to-fifteen feet across. Similar structures housed members of the tribe living in the Russian River Valley and on the shores of Clear Lake. But, as redwood bark was not available to either of these groups, the valley-dwellers substituted willow bark and the Indians of the Clear Lake region used reeds to cover their houses. Meanwhile, the Pomo who roamed California's Central Valley constructed brush shelters or sturdy lean-tos. The latter were often draped with hides wherever deer were abundant.

Besides residences, the Pomo built partially buried earth lodges where religious ceremonies were conducted. They also fashioned a circular building called a *ho hane* (fire lodge). Men took sweat baths, slept, and spent most of their leisure time in the *ho hane*. Women and children slept in the *cha* (living house) which was also used for cooking, eating, and storage.

The Yuroks of northwestern California—who used woodpecker scalps as a medium of exchange—built "split-level" houses. They were made from planks cut out of logs by elk-horn wedges sharpened by rubbing against stones. The wedges were driven into the logs with pear-shaped mauls which the Yuroks fashioned from chunks of basalt (a hard, greenish-black rock of volcanic origin). No other California tribe shaped stone. In fact, the majority lacked building tools.

Yurok houses had porches—large areas in the front flagged with stones. This paved area served as an outdoor living room and was the favorite spot of elderly members of the family, who

Plank house on Salmon River, California (Karok, about 1894)

sat there to sun-bathe and to gossip. As indicated, the house itself was on two levels. This was because the center of its square interior contained a two-to-five foot deep pit outlined with stones. Above the pit, which was used as a fireplace, stood a framework of poles on which fish were dried. The "shelf" surrounding the pit was employed to store provisions and household goods.

Besides residences, Yurok builders constructed sweat houses. These were smaller than dwellings and the interiors were completely excavated, while the side walls did not extend above the ground. Sweat houses were used not only for baths but also as dormitories by men and teen-aged boys.

Like the Yurok, the Hupa built plank houses. But these Indians, who were so isolated that they knew nothing of the whites until they were overrun during the Gold Rush of 1849, covered their dwellings with cedar bark. Hupa villages in the Trinity River Valley were always situated near water and consisted of two types of buildings. The first was a large structure in which women slept and food was stored, while the second was a smaller house where men slept.

Both the Maidu of the Sacramento Valley and the Chumash of the seacoast built circular dwellings. Because these structures housed several families, they were quite large, averaging from twenty to forty feet in diameter. But although both tribes constructed communal shelters of the same shape and size, there was a difference in their building techniques.

Maidu houses were partially underground because they were set in three-foot-deep pits. The house frame was made of poles and logs. These were covered with a very thick layer of earth, which made Maidu dwellings extremely warm.

Chumash house-building was a cooperative effort. All who were to live in the house helped construct it. A circle was first drawn on the ground to mark the structure's circumference; then willow poles were placed close together on the line. When all the poles were in place, their tops were bent toward the center of the circle and lashed together. The building was then covered with mats woven from rushes. Finally, the interior was partitioned so that each family had its own room.

No Indians were more prosperous than those that lived along the Pacific Northwest Coast from northern California to Alaska. All of them were foragers, but they did not have to wander to find food. The sea and the rivers provided them with more than they could use. As a result, the Haida, Kwakiutl, Makah, Nootka, Wishram, and other tribes lived in permanent settlements. Actually, because of their huge stores of food, they could not move about—"even a large family group is unlikely to

Lack of decoration identifies these plank houses as temporary shelters during the salmon-fishing season.

favor a nomadic life if they have half a ton of dried salmon to lug around with them."

Originally, the Indians of the Pacific Northwest lived in huge pit houses that could accommodate 150 people each. The roofs of these dwellings, supported by driftwood poles, were covered by sod and had openings which served as doors and were reached by notched log ladders. Pit-house settlements were always located on the sea shore or along the bank of a river or lake. So were the communities of wooden houses these tribes later constructed.

The wooden houses were from thirty to fifty feet wide and from forty to one hundred feet long. Heavy posts and huge beams were used to make the frame, while the gabled roof and walls consisted of cedar planking. The planks were split from tree trunks with hardwood wedges and joined to the frame by pegs.

Each house sheltered several closely related families. Its owner and his immediate kin resided in the rear left corner. The rest of the occupants lived in the other corners or against the rear wall. Every family had its own fireplace, and also some degree of privacy—the framework of poles on which fish were dried roughly partitioned the interior.

As a general rule, northern tribes built permanent homes. These structures, in which the planking ran vertically, frequently had deep pits near the inside walls arranged like a flight of steps. These were used for storage. The doorway—which always faced a body of water—was a round or oval hole hollowed

Old print shows Pacific Northwest Indians in pit house. Note figure climbing notched log.

John Webber, the artist who accompanied Captain James Cook on his search for the northwest passage, painted this picture of the inside of a house in Nootka Sound.

out of the massive post that rose to the gable. Various symbols denoting the family history of the owner of the house were carved on the post and brilliantly painted. Incidentally, the custom of carving the entrances of their houses motivated the Indians of the Pacific Northwest to erect totem poles depicting the carver's notable experiences, lineage, and rank. Totem-pole making flourished from 1750 when Russian traders brought iron tools into the region until the late nineteenth century. Today, it is almost a lost art.

Southern tribes built houses as attractive as those of their kin in the north. But their dwellings were not so substantial. They were normally constructed so that they could be easily taken apart. This is because their owners visited several different fishing grounds—where they had previously erected house frames

—at various times of the year. The southern tribes notched or grooved roof boards and siding and applied them horizontally, so that a house could be built without the use of pegs. Tying down roofing and siding with flexible twigs served the same purpose. Thus, when a household wanted to move, it was a simple task to strip the framework, carry roof boards and siding to a new campsite, and attach them to another frame.

Plank houses were also built by certain Indians living between the Rocky and Cascade mountain ranges on the high plateau of the Columbia and Fraser rivers. However, the majority of tribes in this region had both summer and winter homes. During the warm months they camped near streams in crude shelters made of poles covered with rush or brush mats. In the fall the Indians moved to sheltered valleys and passed the winter in houses built partially underground and banked with earth to keep out the cold. Because winter houses were frequently communal dwellings, they were often as much as one hundred feet long and twenty feet wide. Each family had its sleeping quarters next to the interior walls and cooked at one of the hearths that were arranged in a row in the center of the room, directly under the smoke hole in the roof.

If the Nez Percé, Cayuse, and other Plateau tribes hadn't acquired the horse, they probably would have continued to build their traditional shelters. But after the introduction of the horse, they adopted the culture and architecture of the Plains Indians who had provided them with their first mounts. As a result, most Plateau-dwellers became buffalo hunters and lived in the most beautiful and practical of all Indian houses—the tepee.

6

"Our fire has gone out, our house is all dark."

The first encounter of Europeans and the Indians of the Great Plains was recorded by Castaneda during Coronado's unsuccessful search for the treasures of Cibola:

> . . . Having proceeded many days through these plains, they came to a settlement of about 200 inhabited houses. The houses were made of the skins of cows, tanned white, like pavilions or army tents. The maintenance or sustance of these Indians comes entirely from the cows, because they neither sow or reap corn. With the skins they make their houses, with the skins they clothe and shoe themselves; of the skin they make rope.

Castaneda was wrong in assuming that all Great Plains tribes lived in "houses made from the skin of cows." Actually, the skin tent known as a tepee only sheltered the Blackfoot, Cheyenne, Comanche, Dakota, and other buffalo (bison) hunting tribes. The Indians of the river valleys on the eastern fringe of the Plains lived in permanent houses while tepees were portable shelters. All the residents of the river valleys—Arikara, Hidatsa, Mandan, and others—were farmers whose settlements were close to their fields.

George Catlin painting of a "Commanche Skin Lodge," 1834. Only bison-hunting Plains tribes used skins for their homes. The Wichita lived in grass lodges, like the one below photographed in 1880. The northern Plains tribes covered their houses with earth to keep out the cold.

"Bird's-eye View of Mandan Village," painted in 1832 by Catlin. The bullboat on the roof of the earth lodge in the foreground was used to cover the smoke hole in rainy weather.

Although there was a slight difference in the way each of the farming tribes constructed their houses, basically all their dwellings were identical. They consisted of a post and rafter frame covered with bark, earth, or grass. The latter was the favorite thatching of the Caddo of the southern Plains whose beehive-like houses were typical of that region. Built with poles lashed together at the top so that they formed a rain-shedding dome, Caddo dwellings resembled the houses of South Sea islanders.

Grass thatching was insulation enough on the southern Plains but it could not keep out the cold of the bitter northern winters. Therefore, northern tribes covered their houses with earth. The Mandan—who probably were the original farmers in the Upper Missouri Valley—built earth lodges that not only accommodated thirty or forty people but also provided storage space for their household goods and hunting and war equipment, as well as shelter for their horses and dogs. "It is," wrote George Catlin, the artist who visited the Mandan early in the nineteenth century, "no uncommon thing to see these lodges fifty feet in diameter inside."

Mandan house-building began with the digging of a circular pit about two feet deep. Poles were then set upright as close together as possible along the circumference of the excavation. Other poles, either notched so that they would fit snugly—the Mandan had no knowledge of wooden pegs—or tied fast to the uprights, formed the domed roof. Sturdy posts, connected to the walls by beams, were raised in the center of the house to provide additional support to the roof.

According to Catlin, the rafters were covered "with a complete mat of willow-boughs of half a foot or more in thickness,

View of a Pawnee earth-lodge village on the Loup Fork, Nebraska, 1871 (William H. Jackson)

which protects the timbers from the dampness of the earth, with which the lodge is covered from bottom to top, to the depth of two or three feet; and then with a hard or tough clay which is impervious to water."

The Mandan spent almost as much time on their rooftops as they did inside their dwellings. Catlin reported that the roof of a Mandan lodge was "a lounging place for the whole family in pleasant weather . . . for wooing lovers . . . a look-out . . . a place for gossip and mirth . . . a seat for solitary gaze and meditation of the stern warrior."

A long tunnel-like entrance led to the lodge's interior. At either end of this passageway, skin curtains were hung to block drafts. Along the sides of the house—whose earth floor had been hardened by flooding it with water and tamping—were horse stalls, storage platforms, and couches that served as seats by day and beds by night. In the center of the lodge directly under the smoke hole—which was framed with branches over which hides were thrown in inclement weather—was a sunken fireplace curbed with stone.

Besides built-in storage platforms, Mandan lodges had "pantries"—bell-shaped excavations under the floor where vegetables were cached. These pits were so deep that they could only be reached by ladders.

The Mandan enclosed their villages of earth-covered, mud-plastered houses with stockades. One of the earliest descriptions of these fortifications appears in the journal kept by Pierre Verendrye, who ranged through the Plains in 1738 seeking the Western Sea. Verendyre mentions seeking six Indian settlements encircled with log palisades and deep ditches.

While these defenses secured the villages from hostile tribes, they offered no protection against the diseases carried by early traders. Thus, by 1837, there were only 150 living Mandan. The rest of the tribe—estimated as some 1,250 individuals by Lewis and Clark—had died from smallpox.

No one knows who made the first tepee. Nor is it possible to trace directly the development of the buffalo-hide tent that became the characteristic shelter of the nomadic mounted hunters of the High Plains. However, it is obvious that the idea of arranging poles so that they formed a conical frame and draping them with hides stemmed from the pole-and-bark houses built by many tribes before they acquired the horse and migrated to the rolling grasslands.

Basically, all tepees were identical, but their appearance and the method of supporting them varied slightly from tribe to tribe. The main difference in construction was in the number of "foundation" poles. Some tribes used three, others four. In either case, after the foundation poles were tied together at their smaller ends, raised, and spread as far apart as possible, ten or more additional poles were leaned against the tilted conical

William Armstrong painted this Blackfoot Indian encampment in the foothills of the Rocky Mountains in the late nineteenth century.

Painting of the Shoshoni war tent of Chief Washakie.

frame to make it stronger. When all the poles were in place, the structure was covered with hides that had been sewn together.

According to Major Stephen H. Long's *Report of an Expedition from Pittsburg to the Rocky Mountains performed in the years 1819 and 1820*, the hides were:

> . . . made fast by one corner to the end of the last pole which is to be raised, by which means it is spread upon the frame with little difficulty. . . . At the summit is a small opening . . . out of which the lodge poles project at some distance, crossing each other at the point where the four shortest are tied together. . . .
>
> When pitched, the skin lodge is of a high conic form; they are comfortable, effectually excluding the rain, and in cold weather a fire is kindled in the centre, the smoke of

which passes through the aperture in the top; on one side of this aperture is a small triangular wing of skin which serves for a cover in rainy weather; and during the rigors of winter to regulate the ascent of the smoke.

The smoke hole wings to which Long refers were attached to movable outside poles. Incidentally, Long's description of smoke flaps is the first mention of them by a white man.

Frequently painted with symbolic designs or representations of the dreams and exploits of their owners, tepees were picturesque. But no Indian dwelling was more practical. Easy to construct, transport, erect, and take down, the tepee was a perfect shelter for nomadic peoples. Moreover, whether bitter cold

A Crow tepee decorated with representations of its owner's dreams and exploits, described in Catlin's account of his adventures on the Great Plains.

winds howled across the Plains, piling snow into tremendous drifts, or the blazing sun burnt the grass and baked the surface of the prairie, the interior of a tepee was always comfortable.

It did not take a big fire to raise the temperature inside a tepee. Its conical shape reduced the volume of air at the top, thus requiring less heat to warm the lower section. Then, too, a "dew cloth"—hides sewn together and attached to the inside of the poles from ground level to shoulder height—served as insulation and kept out both the cold of winter and the heat of the sun.

There was no more difficulty in keeping a tepee cool during the summer as there was in heating it in winter. In the warm months tepees were cross-ventilated by removing the pegs or stones that held down the covering and rolling up the sides.

In short, the Plains Indians "lived within a chimney during the winter and under a parasol during the summer."

Frontiersmen recognized the tepee's efficiency long before General Henry Sibley used it as a model for the tent he designed for the United States Army. When John Frémont asked Kit Carson to guide him through the unmapped West, the famous scout agreed on the condition that the expedition live in tepees. Frémont agreed, but no one in the party including Carson knew how to pitch a tepee. This was because setting up and striking camp was women's work. Fortunately, the expedition met a trader whose Indian wife taught Carson how to erect a tepee.

Not only did women have the responsibility of setting up and taking down tepees but also they designed and made them. This is why the Sioux gave the various parts of their tepees feminine names. While "medicine lodges" belonged to the shamans who used them for ceremonial rites, all other tepees were owned by women. A brave might refer to "my tepee" but all knew it belonged to his wife, who could divorce him by merely throwing

"Encampment of the Piekann Indians." From a painting by Carl Bodmer, 1833

his possessions out the door.

However, men supplied the poles and hides to make tepees. Because the Plains teemed with buffalo, hides were easily obtained. But securing poles on the treeless Plains was difficult. They could be acquired only by traveling long distances to forested regions or by bartering buffalo pelts and meat with woodland tribes that had access to stands of cedar, pine, or tamarack. Incidentally, the larger the tepee, the longer its poles.

Usually, the size of a tepee was determined by the number of people living in it. But all tepees became larger after the Plains Indians became mounted—horses were able to drag longer poles than dogs could. Whether hauled by horse or dog, poles wore down or broke at their ends from being dragged for miles and had to be replaced. Before new poles could be used, the bark had to be removed, their butts pointed so that they could be an-

Indians constructing tepee. Note the four "foundation poles."

chored in the ground, and they had to be seasoned by being set on end to dry. To hasten seasoning, the poles were turned from time to time.

Only straight, smoothly peeled poles were used. This was because Indian women were as ashamed of living in a tepee with crooked or badly trimmed poles as modern housewives are of chipped paint and dirty wallpaper. Then, too, if the poles were bowed, the hide covering would not fit snugly against them.

Every woman hoped to have the honor of setting up the first new tepee when her tribe gathered for its annual summer encampment. But an individual might have to wait years to achieve this goal. If kept in repair, tepee coverings lasted a long time, their lower sections remaining a creamy white—new ones were pure white—while their tops darkened with age. When a tepee could no longer be mended, it was cut up into clothing.

But the coverings of medicine lodges were never used for this purpose. They were ritually destroyed.

The art of tepee-making was passed from mother to daughter in most tribes, but Cheyenne girls received their instruction from a guild. In addition to teaching, the women of the guild gave parties where they bragged of their ability to make tepees, just as warriors boasted of their victories at councils. Meanwhile, in certain other tribes, women placed an incised dot on the handles of their tanning tools to signify that they had either made ten tepees or prepared one hundred pelts.

Although the how-to of tepee construction was common knowledge—children made tepees for their puppies from leaves

Flathead Indians preparing a meal in front of a modern "tepee." Incidentally, this tribe never artificially flattened their heads, but were given the name by French traders who saw slaves owned by them who had deformed heads.

and twigs—Plains Indian women had good reason to be proud of their skill. It took considerable strength and much patience to prepare the hides for a tepee covering. Not only did all the hair and flesh have to be removed from a pelt but also it had to be dried, cured, and made pliable.

Tanning the hides, making a "pattern" (stakes in the ground), and sewing the covering together was a cooperative effort. The married women and maidens who worked on a new tepee were supervised by a respected woman of the tribe. Besides overseeing, she sewed the smoke flaps. This task could only be done by a woman of high moral character as it was believed that "Wicked women's sewing makes the smoke go back into the tepee"—and no one wanted the dwellings filled with smoke every time a fire was lit.

However, a new tepee was filled with smoke before being occupied. The smoke hole was fastened down, causing the smoke to impregnate the covering. This waterproofed the hides and kept them from becoming hard and stiff after exposure to rain.

Interiors of tepees were as colorful as their exteriors. Decorations hung from the poles and dew cloths were embroidered or painted. But furnishings were few—the more household goods a family owned, the heavier the load for their horses. While the Blackfoot and the Crow had backrests made of willow withes and Arapaho tepees were fitted with beds raised above the ground, other Plains Indians sat and slept on buffalo robes.

Originally, tepee doors—which always faced away from the prevailing winds—were merely hides or old blankets stretched across wooden frames. But over the years, doors became one of the most attractive parts of a tepee and were painted, quilled, or beaded. An open door was an invitation to visit, but would-be guests knew that no one was home or that a family wished to be alone if the door was crossed by two sticks.

74

Painting of a feast honoring representatives of the Great White Father, by Catlin. Note how two tepees have been joined to shelter all the guests.

When the door was closed, callers were expected to cry out, knock on the side of the tepee, or shake the deer-hoof rattle that hung at the entrance. Once inside, a male visitor went to the northern side of the tepee and sat down with his legs either crossed or outstretched. Women guests sat on the south side with their legs tucked under them.

75

The only time a Blackfoot mother entered a married daughter's tepee was when her son-in-law was away. But Sioux suitors never saw the interior of the dwelling of their loved ones. A maiden received her admirers in the doorway. Although a chaperon stood directly behind the girl, courting couples ignored her—they wrapped themselves in a blanket and drew it over their heads for privacy.

In 1599, after returning from an expedition across present Oklahoma and Kansas, Don Juan de Onate noted that "The Indians . . . are as well sheltered in their tents as they could be in any house." Modern anthropologists agree but argue about which Plains tribe fashioned the most comfortable and attractive tepees. But there is no debate as to when and where the most unusual tepees were built, or who made them. Following the massacre of Custer's troops at the Little Big Horn on June 25, 1876, the children of the victorious Sioux and Cheyenne warriors made miniature tepees with the money taken from the pockets of the dead soldiers.

7

"Houses are built to live in, not to look on..."

Many people call any Indian dwelling, whether earth lodge, pole-and-thatch hut, tepee, or wickiup, a "wigwam." This is incorrect. The term wigwam—an Algonquian word meaning house—only applies to the dwellings constructed by red men living along the Atlantic seaboard, by certain northern nomads, and by the Chippewa and other tribes who made seasonal journeys to gather fruit, nuts, seeds, and maple sap.

There are two other common misconceptions about wigwams. The first is that all wigwams were covered with birch bark; the second, that wigwams were always conical in shape. As a matter of fact, many wigwams were covered with reed mats or thatching. However, birch bark was preferred by Indians who employed bark. This was because it is very easy to peel. But when birch was not available, elm, hemlock, or spruce bark was used.

Similarly, while conical wigwams were common, domed ones were also constructed. Others resembled arbors. The *sidiken* (bough house) of the Penobscot was typical of the latter type. It was made by laying evergreen boughs with their tips hanging downward on a frame and placing poles against them to hold them in place.

Actually, there is little architectural difference between a conical wigwam and a tepee. Approximately ten feet in diameter

and ten feet tall at its peak, a wigwam consists of a framework of peeled cedar or spruce poles over which a covering is placed and kept tight against the frame by unpeeled poles.

When constructing a wigwam, the builder tied the four foundation poles together with cedar bark about two feet from their tops and set the four on end. He then placed other poles between the foundation ones so that they strengthened the frame. A lintel (horizontal support) fashioned from a hoop of flexible wood linked the poles on the inside.

If bark was used as a covering, it was applied in sheets about three-and-one-half feet wide sewn into long strips with spruce roots. However, bark sheets were not sewn together for a temporary camp. They were laid over the frame and held down with poles of varying lengths.

Three tiers of bark strips enclosed a conical wigwam. The first tier was fastened to a door post of the frame and the bark was carried around to the middle pole in the back and tied down. The same procedure was followed with the second tier. Instead

Left top: Chippewa camp at Mille Lac, Minnesota, showing two types of bark lodges

Left bottom: Note arrangement of "door" on this birch-bark wigwam photographed in Canada.

Right: Similar in construction to the birch-bark wigwams of eastern North America, this northwestern hut is covered with mats.

of attaching the third tier to a door post, it was fastened at its upper edge to the rear pole. Then it was looped completely around the frame until its ends overlapped and could be joined. The opening between the top of the third tier and the intersection of the poles formed the smoke hole.

Once the bark was in place, the outside poles, which were about ten feet long, were laid on it. To make sure the poles would not slip, their butts were anchored in the ground and their tops tied with withes to an inside pole just above the top tier of bark.

No wigwams were more quickly set up than those used by the Chippewa bands who trekked from one shallow body of water to another harvesting wild rice every autumn. These Indians lived in dome-shaped wigwams fashioned from saplings and covered with long, wide strips of birch bark. When all the *manimin* (good berry) was picked from a pond, the women stripped the bark off the sapling frames, rolled it up, and carried it to another campsite.

Although log cabins were unknown to the Indians—they were introduced into the New World in 1638 by Swedish settlers— some New England tribes laid logs crossways to form the lower section of their square or rectangular wigwams. The logs were chinked with moss and banked with earth to keep out the cold.

The Narragansett, Micmac, and other tribes that fished and hunted along the northeastern seaboard dwelt in wigwam villages while camping at their summer fishing grounds and after their annual fall deer hunt. Their dome-shaped shelters were formed by setting saplings in the ground, bending them over, and tying their tops together. Bulrushes, cattails, bark, or woven mats fastened with roots or pegs were used to cover the frames. Meanwhile, certain of the "slash-and-burn" farming tribes living nearby were building long, barrack-like, multi-family dwellings and one-family residences with poles and brush.

Reconstructed Wampanoag summer house at Plimoth Plantation, Massachusetts

Some tribes who camped along the waterways of the northeast incorporated their canoes into their houses of poles and evergreen boughs when winter approached. The canoes were inverted and placed on the windward side of the house to break the force of the wind. Jacques Cartier, discoverer of the St. Lawrence River, saw so many houses employing canoes for windbreaks that he thought the Indians built no other type of dwelling. He discovered his error when he visited Hochelaga, a large Indian village on the site of modern Montreal.

The residents of Hochelaga were of Iroquoin stock—a group of Indians native to the eastern sections of the United States and

Canada who spoke similar languages. Many of these tribes had the same culture. Although they hunted and fished, they never wandered very far from their villages, which were located near their fields of beans, corn, and squash. When the fertility of the soil was exhausted and all the easily gathered firewood consumed, these Indians moved to another site.

Originally, most of the semi-agricultural tribes of the eastern woodlands lived in "beehive" huts made of peeled poles bent in an arc, braced by a diagonal support, and lashed together. The poles were covered with bark strips, grass, or mats. Eventually, the beehive hut evolved into the "longhouse." This distinctive bark-covered structure—one of the highest forms of architecture created by northern Indians—was perfected by the Iroquois. Actually, the Iroquois is not the name of a tribe but a composite name for the Mohawk, Oneida, Onondaga, Cayuga, Seneca, and the tribes they adopted.

Francis Parkman, a famous historian, called the Iroquois "the Romans of the New World." He had good reason. No North American Indians equaled them in political organization, ability to govern, or as warriors. One of their greatest achievements was to form an organization in 1570 comparable to the United Nations. This confederation established laws that insured punishment for "practically every offence against peace, well-being, and order."

"The People of the Longhouse" resided along the Mohawk River and west through central New York State in villages where the populations ranged from three hundred to three thousand. The majority of these settlements were fortified. Some of the larger communities were protected by double or triple rings of upright, sharply pointed logs and deep ditches. Within the stockades, longhouses were built in rows.

Longhouses were rectangular, twenty to thirty feet wide and fifty to one hundred feet long, with barrel-like roofs. They were

Bark longhouse of the Iroquois

also much higher than the huts from which they developed. After visiting a group of Indians living in beehive huts, a trader reported that the entrances to the huts "were so small that they had to stoop down and squeeze themselves to get through them." But longhouses—which were twenty feet tall—had wide doors.

Most of the construction of a longhouse was done by women. Moreover, with the exception of buildings reserved for civil ceremonies and religious rites, all longhouses belonged to the women who lived in them. Husbands were treated as honored guests as long as they provided game for food and hides for

Note the clay-chinked log cabin behind this modern Iroquois longhouse.

clothing. If they failed to do so, they were evicted.

As many as twenty families lived in a longhouse. The structure's interior was partitioned at intervals of six to twenty feet, depending upon its size. As a result, each family had a stall-like open area that faced a passageway running the length of the building. An entrance at each end of this corridor was covered with a skin curtain or a bark door.

In the center of the passageway was a series of fireplaces. Each was located so that it could serve four families—two on either side of the corridor. Thus a longhouse with five fireplaces contained twenty "apartments," which were furnished with raised bunks around their three sides. If all the partitioned areas were not occupied, the empty ones were used for storage.

Not only did longhouses shelter the Iroquois but also they played an important part in their traditions. In fact, the Iroquois visualized themselves as "dwelling in a large long house which had a door at the eastern end guarded by the Mohawk . . . and a door on the western end guarded by the Seneca."

Long before the War Between the States, the Five Civilized Tribes (Cherokee, Chickasaw, Choctaw, Creek, and Seminole) living in eastern Oklahoma had adopted the architecture of the white man. However, most other Indians continued to build houses as they had always done until they were forced onto reservations and misguided government officials attempted to wipe out their age-old culture.

Today, few Indians live in the traditional dwelling of their tribe. To be sure, certain pueblos still teem with life, hogans dot the canyons of the Southwest, and council fires burn brightly in the longhouses of the Iroquois. But the tepees pitched at rodeos and on the outskirts of certain National Parks are merely tourist attractions. So are the numerous "Indian villages" clustered along major highways. Moreover, many of the Indians who gather wild rice travel from pond to pond in a "Camper" and have no idea how to build a birch-bark wigwam.

Fortunately, in recent years young adults whose grandparents chose to follow the white man's road are displaying a keen interest in their tribal history and culture. As a result, old customs and forgotten skills have been revived. It is, of course, most unlikely that any modern red men will construct a ceremonial center like Chichén Itzá or raise a huge pyramidal flat-topped mound and set a wood-and-wattle temple on it. But if the young men and women of Indian descent continue their efforts, the building techniques of their ancestors will not be forgotten.

Meanwhile, although the red man made no major contribution to house-building, he plays a vital role in modern architecture. Whenever a high bridge is constructed or a towering skyscraper erected in the United States, the chances are that the girders are being handled by Indians. These sure-footed tribesmen are considered the finest steel workers in the world.

Index

About the Author

Sigmund A. Lavine was highly active while in college; he wrote features for the *Boston Sunday Post* and covered Boston University sports for two wire services. After receiving his M.A., he taught in a United States Government Indian School at Belcourt, North Dakota, for two years, learned to speak both the Sioux and Cree languages and talk in sign language. He was invited to tribal dances, ceremonies, and Indian Court in reservations throughout Canada and the Northwest.

Sigmund Lavine has taught in the Boston schools for over thirty years and is now an assistant principal. He also lectures and writes literary criticism.

With his wife—and a whippet answering to the unlikely name of Morrisey, the latest in a long line of prize-winning dogs owned by the Lavines—he lives in a house filled with books, fish tanks, historical china, art glass, and the largest privately owned collection of Gilbert and Sullivan material in America. For relaxation the Lavines attend country auctions, go "antiquing," or browse in bookstores, but their greatest pleasure is truck gardening on a piece of rocky New Hampshire land.